Original title:
Garden Secrets

Copyright © 2025 Creative Arts Management OÜ
All rights reserved.

Author: William Hawthorne
ISBN HARDBACK: 978-1-80566-753-7
ISBN PAPERBACK: 978-1-80566-823-7

The Buried Palette

In pots of paint, they thought they'd find,
A rainbow feast for eyes so blind.
But squirrels stole brushes, oh what a sight!
Now walls are pink, and grass is white!

The daisies giggle, the roses play tricks,
They claim the weeds are both smart and slick.
While marigolds mutter in hues of despair,
"It's a color war; we never signed up for this affair!"

Hushed Whispers of the Soil

The earth below has tales to spill,
Of worms who dance and frogs who thrill.
With dirt mustaches and roots that tease,
They throw wild parties with ravenous bees!

Along came a snail, he glided so slow,
With secrets of slugs, on slippery, they'd grow.
"We'll keep it down, just us and the ants,
Let's shimmy and shake in our muddy pants!"

The Secrets of Nectar

Buzzing with gossip, the bees took flight,
In search of sweet whispers, they buzzed with delight.
"Who stole the sugar?" they shouted in glee,
As butterflies flitted, like confetti in tea!

The flowers all blushed, they held their own news,
A petal parade with colorful hues.
"Don't let the humans know what we share,
They'll dip in our honey, like they're unaware!"

Beneath the Blossoms

Beneath the blooms, the critters conspire,
To munch on the petals with snack-time desire.
"I'm not a thief, just a taster of dreams,
This flower pizza is bursting at the seams!"

With suns sparkling down, they joked without pause,
"We'll form a band, call ourselves 'The Paws!'
We'll dance and sing till the dusk sweeps in,
And let the moonlight sprinkle us thin!"

The Leafy Confession

In the shade where critters dwell,
A ladybug spilled all to a shell.
"I once danced on a daisy bright,
But slipped and tumbled in broad daylight!"

The carrot chuckled, roots all aglow,
"You think that's funny? Let me show!
I wiggle and jiggle, then dig so deep,
I dream of the salad that I can't keep!"

Enchanted Roots

Beneath the soil, the garlic yells,
"I smell betrayal from nearby smells!
If onions cry, what's to become,
Of this sautéed fate—oh, here they come!"

A playful beet chimes in with glee,
"You all are just too green for me!
I thrive on jokes, puns, and mirth,
But watch your step, I own this earth!"

Echoes of the Herbarium

A sprig of thyme told tales so wild,
Of a rogue spinach, once a child.
"He hid in shadows, of that I'm sure,
Until he sprouted, brave and pure!"

Then parsley chimed in with a scoff,
"Oh please, dear thyme, don't set me off!
I've seen the craziness of a dill,
Who thought he could roll down the hill!"

The Secret Scroll of Flora

There's a scroll tucked behind the fence,
Filled with whispers and laughter so dense.
It tells of daisies with wild dreams,
Who twirled under moonlight and burst at the seams!

A hidden club, by clovers defined,
Where gossip blooms, and puns unwind.
With petals as hats and roots as chairs,
They giggle and dance without any cares!

The Essence of Forgotten Flora

In a corner, weeds do jest,
Hiding treasures, birdies nest.
Pansies gossip, quite absurd,
Telling tales of a lost bird.

Dandelions play hide and seek,
With every puff, they giggle and peek.
A flower pot that thinks it's grand,
Wishes for a rock band.

Bees throw parties, buzzing loud,
While ants parade, oh so proud.
A snail wears shades, looking sleek,
Sipping dew; he'll never speak.

Tulips tease the passing breeze,
"Blow us kisses, if you please!"
Amidst the blooms, it's all a show,
Just wait until the tomatoes grow!

Whispers Through the Lavender

Lavender sways with flair and glee,
Whispering secrets to the bee.
"Hey there, buddy! Try my scent,
But if too much, you might get bent!"

Chives conspire with the mint,
"Let's trip the cat, it's time to sprint!"
With every snip, the scents collide,
And every critter tries to hide.

Petunias croon their nightly tune,
Frogs and crickets dance by the moon.
"Join our cabaret, don't be shy,
But watch out for that sly old fly!"

Basil laughs, says, "Life's a feast,
Grab a slice of pie, at least!"
Through tangled leaves, the stories flow,
In this place where laughter grows.

Elysium Within the Thorns

In a thicket, roses pout,
"We're the queens, no doubt about!"
But prickly weeds just roll their eyes,
"Who needs crowns? We're full of surprise!"

Thistles joke, with pointed pride,
"Join our club, take that wild ride!"
With every poke, they get a laugh,
As daisies dance, forming a raft.

A dragonfly spins dizzy tales,
While ladybugs don tiny veils.
The butterflies throw a fête in flight,
Under stars that twinkle bright.

So heed the call, and join the cheer,
For nature's whims bring us near.
In every corner, jesters play,
Where laughter blooms, come what may!

The Art of Blooming Silence

In the corner, gnomes stand still,
They whisper tales of bending will.
A flower blushes, no one's around,
Yet giggles echo from the ground.

With muddy paws and secret sights,
The rabbits host wild, silent nights.
They burrow deep, with snacks they pry,
While moles are dancing, oh my, oh my!

Butterflies wear polka dots and stripes,
Telling stories of their silly types.
A petal slips, it trips, it falls,
And cactus laughs at plants' dull brawls.

Oh, the calm chaos blooms each day,
Where even weeds have words to say.
Nature's whimsy hides in plain view,
Capering beneath the sky so blue.

A Tapestry of Life

In the patchwork of colors bright,
Silly bugs dance in morning light.
A ladybug dons her tiny crown,
While worms wiggle, never frown.

The daisies gossip with the breeze,
Swapping secrets with utmost ease.
A busy bee, with pockets full,
Is chatted up by a honeyed hull.

Sunflowers do the twist and sway,
While shadows play a funny sway.
In this patch of joy so spry,
Laughter lingers as squirrels fly.

Every leaf has a bizarre tale,
Of stolen hats or a snail's mail.
In the wild weave of nature's art,
It's good to know we all take part.

Alchemy of the Seed

When seeds conspire underground,
They plot their rise without a sound.
A stubborn sprout, with dreams so grand,
Yearns for the sun, to make a stand.

The rain drops laugh, a playful shower,
While roots stretch forth in hidden power.
Each tiny bulb wears a mischievous grin,
Waiting for spring's warm day to begin.

A pumpkin fancies itself a star,
While carrots giggle, "Look at that far!"
Potatoes argue over who's best,
While herbs just roll with merry jest.

In this world of leafy play,
Nature's roguish tricks hold sway.
From tiny seeds to mighty trees,
It's chaos shared with lightest ease.

The Quiet Thrum of Nature

Beneath the surface, chaos hums,
As critters plot their tiny sums.
The frogs croak bass, with notes so loud,
While crickets chirp, feeling proud.

A playful breeze steals leaves away,
In shadows where the fungi play.
The mushrooms chuckle, dressed up nice,
While thorns roll jokes, rather precise.

Squirrels compete on acorn race,
Fumbling fits with no trace of grace.
A wise old owl grins from a tree,
As squirrels trip, and fall with glee.

This silence isn't quiet, you see,
It's laughter wrapped in grassy glee.
In nature's thrum, the jokes abound,
In every nook, mirth can be found.

The Language of Flora

In the chatter of bloom, they speak so loud,
Whispers of petals among the proud.
Daisies giggle, and roses tease,
Telling tales on a gentle breeze.

The tulips jest with their colorful caps,
While sunflowers nod like silly chaps.
They conspire under the sun's warm glow,
Plotting surprises only they know.

Violets scheme behind the leafy wall,
With pansies laughing at the butterflies' crawl.
Every stalk has its most humorous part,
Blooming jests from nature's heart.

So if you listen, you might just find,
The jokes and gags that plants unwind.
In a world where roots wiggle and sway,
Life's a laugh in a different way.

Shadows of the Fern

Beneath the fronds, the playful shade,
A hide-and-seek game in leafy glade.
Ferns wear hats of the finest green,
And giggle softly, oh what a scene!

They shuffle silently, the whispers reign,
Telling tales as they dance in the rain.
Mossy cushions beneath a tangled mess,
They snicker at clovers all in distress.

Roots like fingers, they wiggle and squirm,
Encouraging daisies to stand firm.
Those mischievous greens have stories to tell,
With every leap, they cast a spell.

So wander close and listen in tight,
To the shadows of ferns at the fall of night.
In their secret world of glee and fun,
Every leaf revels, every stem runs!

Moonlight and Marigolds

Under the glow of the silver light,
Marigolds pirouette in delight.
They shake their petals in a cosmic dance,
Trying to catch the stars in a glance.

With crickets as DJs, the night's a blast,
A lamp-lit soiree, it's quite the contrast.
Frogs in tuxedos croak out the tune,
While ladybugs sway in the evening's croon.

The moon winks down, enjoying the sight,
Of flowers and critters having their bite.
A comedy show with no audience near,
Except for a mouse cracking jokes by the pier.

So if you're awake on a clear night peak,
You might hear marigolds starting to speak.
In the dance of the dark, they find a way,
To make the mundane just a bit of play.

Echoes in the Arbor

Beneath the trellis, the whispers roam,
Branches sharing secrets of their home.
The bees play tag, and the squirrels debate,
About who gets to choose the best mate.

Every twig has a quip on the breeze,
While apples chuckle from their leafy trees.
The shadows dance in hilarious forms,
Sketching drawings during chilly storms.

A laughing woodpecker pecks with delight,
Telling tales of his day in the spotlight.
And the jolly oak just shrugs and sways,
Adding its thoughts in mysterious ways.

So listen closely to the chatter and roar,
Where the echoes in the arbor leave you wanting more.
Amid the rustling and giggles that flee,
Lies a funny story, come take a seat!

Echoes of the Hidden Grove

In a patch where daisies play,
Worms dance like they own the day.
Whispers of mischief fill the air,
Toadstools giggle without a care.

Bees wear tiny sunglasses bright,
Buzzing tunes, oh what a sight!
Squirrels gossip in their trees,
As the wind plays tricks with ease.

A rabbit's peek from leafy shade,
Picks out carrots—oh, the trade!
With a wink and a twitchy nose,
It steals a snack, and off it goes.

Underneath a sunbeam's glow,
Frogs tell tales of high and low.
While ladybugs laugh, red and bright,
In the hidden grove, all is right.

Twilight's Embrace

At dusk, the fireflies take their stand,
With little lights, they form a band.
Crickets chirping, quite the show,
As shadows dance, they steal the glow.

A raccoon in a hat so wide,
Steals the snacks, but tries to hide.
With popcorn kernels in his paws,
He's the thief without a pause.

The moon peeks in with a smirk,
While owls plot their nighttime work.
"Whooo's that?" a squirrel seems to say,
As shadows play and scurry away.

In this twilight, laughter's bright,
As critters roam, ready for a bite.
With secrets shared in this dark place,
Each night ends in a comical chase.

Beneath the Canopy

Underneath those branches wide,
Monkeys swing, oh what a ride!
Laughing leaves tickle their toes,
While wise old owls watch their shows.

A hedgehog wears a tiny hat,
Waddling proud, imagine that!
With every droll and little smile,
He struts along in endless style.

Ants march in a straight parade,
Carrying crumbs they deftly made.
"Hey, move aside!" the beetles cry,
While hiding from a hungry pie.

The sunlight peeks in, full of glee,
As all the flowers shake their spree.
Each petal giggles, freely sway,
Beneath the canopy, they play.

The Watchful Fern

In a corner, ferns stand tall,
With watchful eyes, they catch it all.
Yet one is known for mischief keen,
Pulls pranks on those who tread unseen.

A snail drags slowly, quite a sight,
Challenging ferns to a race at night.
"Oh look," they whisper, "What a show!"
As the clever snail moves slow.

Mice sneak past, tiptoeing light,
While ferns giggle, feeling bright.
"No entrance here!" the ferns declare,
As they trip unwitting guests with flair.

In this realm of leafy fun,
Where secrets hide and laughter's spun,
The watchful fern keeps tales so sly,
In the leafy world where critters fly.

The Scent of Forgotten Things

In the pot where soup was brewed,
Lies a sock, previously chewed.
Forgotten herbs, all turned to dust,
Mixed with laughter, oh, what a fuss!

A garden gnome without his hat,
Claims he saw a dancing cat.
Sunflower seeds with wild old tales,
Of sneaky squirrels and stolen males!

Beneath the patch of prickly greens,
Are buried treasures, or so it seems.
Rusty tools and broken spades,
Sticky fingers of leafy parades!

With every bloom, a secret's spun,
Nature's pranks are never done.
The scent of oddities fills the air,
In this circus of blooms, a clown's lair!

Leaves of Lament

Once a leaf with dreams so grand,
Fell from high, couldn't withstand.
Now it laughs, a crispy throng,
Joining whispers, joining song.

Underneath the faded rose,
Weeds weave tales nobody knows.
A dandelion just won't quit,
Declaring, 'I'm too bright to sit!'

Yet in the shade of swinging swings,
Gossip of forgotten kings.
Once a throne of dainty vines,
Now a seat for wayward signs.

And all around, the petals sigh,
Wishing dreams could learn to fly.
Leaves may fall, but oh, they play,
In the dance of night and day!

Mysteries in Sunlit Corners

In the corner where shadows creep,
Lies a secret that won't sleep.
A lingering smell of pickle brine,
Amidst the herbs, it's quite divine!

Whispers of a hedgehog's plight,
Searching for snacks late at night.
Caught in a sunflower's embrace,
He finds himself in a silly race.

The carrots plot a leafy coup,
While tomatoes giggle in a stew.
Lettuce leaves in turtleneck sprout,
Gathering gossip like it's a bout!

And just nearby, a ladybug,
Is plotting her best little shrug.
"My life's a drama, come and see,
A soap opera, oh woe is me!"

Cradled in Blossom's Veil

Beneath a petal's gentle sway,
A bunny dreams of yesterday.
He twitches in his floral bed,
Wearing daisies on his head.

A butterfly with colores bold,
Tells tales of treasures made of gold.
"I saw a snail in a fancy car,
Zooming past like a superstar!"

The tulips giggle, sharing jokes,
About the silliness of folks.
"Why did the sunflower stop to stare?
He thought his shadow had no hair!"

In this realm where whimsy thrives,
Every flower has clever jives.
Cradled in the warmth of glee,
Nature's humor is plain to see!

Embrace of the Morning Mist

In the dawn, the dew drops dance,
Whispering tales of last night's prance.
Bumblebees stumble, quite the sight,
Chasing dreams in the soft daylight.

Mice wear hats made of mushroom caps,
While the daisies sing, oh, such mishaps!
Frogs in bow ties croak with glee,
Bidding good morning, wild and free.

The snails carry homes that sparkle bright,
Engaging in races, oh, what a fright!
Each leaf holds a joke wrapped tight,
In the misty morn, laughter takes flight.

A squirrel reads maps, thinks he's a sage,
Chasing his tail in a comedic rage.
Morning mist giggles with every breeze,
Nature's humor always aims to please.

Conversations with the Sunflower

Oh sunflower, tall and proud you stand,
Do you really understand this land?
'You bet!' she beams, 'I see it all!
A wiggle moves, the grass does call!'

With petals bright, she spins a tale,
Of bees wearing shoes and a cat on a rail.
'Last week, I saw a rabbit in socks,
He danced with the moon and the funny old box!'

'Then there was Gertrude, the parakeet,
She painted her beak and can't be beat!
She cackled and laughed, oh what a scene,
Flirting with clouds, so cheeky and keen.'

They speak of laughter, in colors so bold,
'Tell me your secrets, the stories untold!'
With each sunny glance, a giggle's unfurled,
In the patch of warmth, where joy's always swirled.

The Lore of Earthly Delights

Mysteries brewed in a teapot of clay,
With whispers of radishes having their day.
Carrots wear crowns, oh what a sight!
Eating their cake with pure delight.

Tomatoes twist tales of love and woe,
Who knew they could act in a show?
Peas and beans play peek-a-boo,
As laughter erupts from the earthy crew.

'Listen close!' chirp the beans in fun,
'We've seen the sun shine, we've kissed the run!
You won't believe what the rhubarb said,
It's planning a party with grapes and bread!'

When the moon glows, the radishes sing,
Each root a storyteller, blooming in spring.
In the lore of delights, they dance with glee,
Making merry at the moonlit spree.

Secrets Curling in the Leaves

Under the canopy, whispers abound,
Trees are the keepers, secrets unbound.
Leaves start to gossip, they ruffle and sway,
'Did you hear what the owl had to say?'

A fern rolled its eyes, 'Oh, do tell fast!
I heard he wore glasses, making shadows cast.'
While the thistle proclaimed with a puffed up chest,
'In the world of secrets, I am the best!'

Dandelions chuckled, 'We're not just for show,
We've hosted great battles, you just don't know!'
Each petal a tale, every wind a sigh,
In the hush of the woods, the laughter won't die.

So here in the shade, with giggles that float,
Nature spills secrets, a cheerful devote.
Each leaf is a page in this funny old book,
Curling in joy, let's take a look!

The Dance of Unseen Creatures

In the shadows, something stirs,
A squirrel twirls, the dance occurs.
With tiny leaps, and silly spins,
It steals a nut, and laughs at sins.

The earthworms wiggle, who'd have guessed?
They hold a rave, oh what a fest!
With disco lights and mud for floor,
The garden rocks, we beg for more.

A rabbit hops, it leads the way,
While ladybugs join in the play.
They twirl and twist, both bold and bright,
Under the moon, they own the night.

So here's to life, in every nook,
Where creatures join, and no one looks.
In hidden realms, the jesters thrive,
In secret dances, we come alive!

Echoes of the Bumblebee

Buzzing loudly, like a song,
A bumblebee can't do much wrong.
It sips from flowers, sweet as pie,
Then claims it's full, but still wants more pie!

With polka dots upon its rear,
It wiggles past without a fear.
It chases friends, who just can't see,
That life's a game, oh, silly bee!

A daisy says, "Please take your time,"
While dandelions laugh in rhyme.
They whisper jokes, as bees take flight,
And dance beneath the golden light.

So when you hear that buzzing sound,
Just know the fun is all around.
In every flower, joy will swell,
In all the stories they'll retell!

The Heart's Green Lullaby

At twilight's fall, the leaves do sway,
Whispering tales of the day.
A frog croaks loud—a mellow beat,
As crickets join, a serenade sweet.

The daffodils nod in soft delight,
As moonlight waltzes through the night.
They giggle softly in the air,
While shadows dance without a care.

A sleepy cat curls up, it seems,
In her dreams, she chases beams.
The stars above just wink and glow,
As nature hums its gentle flow.

So close your eyes, let laughter steer,
In whispers shared with all you hear.
The heart of night, a lullaby,
That holds us close, as time slips by!

Whispers of the Willow

The willow sways with stories old,
In laughter's arms, it sings so bold.
Its branches whisper secrets near,
Of wayward winds and squirrels' cheer.

A crow caws loud, it joins the jest,
A feathered friend, not one to rest.
With jokes that tickle ev'ry leaf,
The garden flares with comic relief.

Beneath the shade, the rabbits plot,
In search of snacks that hit the spot.
They giggle low, then sneak away,
With crisp delights they munch and play.

So gather 'round the willow's shade,
Where laughter grows and shyness fades.
In every whisper, cheer abounds,
In nature's heart, joy can be found!

The Enchanted Thicket

In the thicket where daisies giggle,
Rabbits wear ties and jump with a wiggle.
Squirrels throw acorns, aiming for fun,
While turtles race fast, but only for one.

A hedgehog's party, they dance and they prance,
With mushrooms for chairs, they all take a stance.
Ladybugs gossip on petals so sly,
As frogs croon sweet tunes beneath the blue sky.

A dandelion crown on a shy bumblebee,
As he bumbles about, sipping nectar with glee.
The wind joins in, tickling leaves all around,
And the laughter of critters is the sweetest sound.

So if you meander through ferns and through brambles,
Know that magic resides where adventure scrambles.
Just keep your secrets, no need to confide,
In this whimsical world where silliness hides.

Secrets Beneath the Soil

Worms plot the garden, they whisper and scheme,
As cabbages chuckle, lost in a dream.
Beneath all the roots, there's a wild parade,
With beetles and bugs in a crunchy charade.

A potato winks as it's dug from the earth,
While carrots sing songs of their underground birth.
All the radishes hide, with their tops in a dance,
Planting seeds of mischief with each little chance.

Under the soil, the gossip does flow,
About insects that dance in the moon's gentle glow.
They giggle and snicker at flowers so bright,
Hiding their secrets from the curious night.

So if you're a wanderer, take heed of the ground,
For the silliness hidden is waiting, profound.
Beneath every leaf, and each clump of clay,
Lives a world of laughter that's ready to play.

Serpentines of Serenity

In a winding path where the lilies entwine,
A snail holds the map, he thinks he's divine.
Tangled up vines offer shade and a chill,
While chameleons flirt with their jazzy green thrill.

Butterflies float like they own the sweet air,
Trading their colors, a whimsical flair.
With daisies and poppies all forming a crew,
They throw a parade just to brighten the view.

A lazy old tortoise plays catch with a rock,
He swears it's a ball as he gives it a knock.
In the midst of the fun, a shadowy squirrel,
Leaves a nut in the court, making everyone twirl.

And as twilight descends with a twinkle and sigh,
The critters all gather, the jokes flying high.
In the serpentines sleeping under the moon,
Cutting loose and laughing, it's quite the festoon!

Crickets' Midnight Confession

At the stroke of the night, with a chirp and a hop,
The crickets confess with a rapturous stop.
They sing of their crushes on fireflies bright,
Who flicker and giggle in the warm, starry light.

A toad sings a tune, a passionate croak,
As the moon winks down with a playful poke.
It's a raucous affair, with a glee-filled refrain,
While owls look on, trying hard to maintain.

The secrets they share are both silly and sweet,
Like dancing on blades of soft green, cool wheat.
In whispers, they giggle of bug love gone wrong,
How one got stuck in a grasshopper song.

So next time you hear them, just listen and laugh,
For the tales they spin take a silly old path.
In the heart of the night, with their laughter in tune,
The crickets confess under the light of the moon.

Colored Shadows

In a patch where daisies dance,
The sun plays tricks and takes a chance.
A bluebird wears a yellow hat,
While kittens plot to catch a rat.

Beehives hum a silly tune,
As ants march home beneath the moon.
With ladybugs in polka dot,
They gossip 'bout the flowers' plot.

The carrots giggle, hiding deep,
While flowers trade their secrets cheap.
But squirrels toss acorns with a cheer,
Making sure the gossip's clear.

So if you stop and take a peek,
You'll find that vegetables can speak.
In this place of laughter and delight,
Even shadows dance in bright sunlight.

Chasing the Butterflies' Tale

A moth once claimed she knew it all,
Of scents and colors, big and small.
But butterflies just rolled their eyes,
And clashed their wings with soft goodbyes.

They flit and flutter, zigzagging round,
While crickets lend a rhythmic sound.
A snail, quite slow, just shakes his head,
While worms debate on where they'll spread.

Chasing tails, they twirl and spin,
Hiding from the beetles' grin.
In search of nectar, oh what fun,
They play all day under the sun.

But little did they know this weed,
Was plotting something quite absurd indeed!
It laughed and wrapped around their feet,
"Tag, you're it!" it cried, "A funny treat!"

In the Thicket of Memories

In a bramble thick with stories told,
A gopher dreams of treasures bold.
His thoughts are deeper than his hole,
While moles sing songs without a goal.

A squirrel's debate on acorn fate,
While beetles boast of love and hate.
They argue over who is best,
And laugh about their nightly quest.

Old twigs whisper of lovebirds' chime,
As ferns recall the dance in rhyme.
Each leaf a page, each root a line,
In memories where creatures dine.

But if you linger for a trace,
You might just see the worm's wise face.
He'll wink and say, "Oh, join the spree,
For laughter grows in every tree."

Unseen Shades of Green

In a patch of clovers, what do we see?
A gnome who's lost his way to tea.
He trips on roots and bumps his nose,
While laughing vines untangle woes.

The peppers gossip, oh so bold,
While radishes share tales of old.
Each twist and turn, a funny blight,
As pumpkins grow with pure delight.

Yet hidden there, a frog does croak,
Saying, "Did you hear the latest joke?"
With every leap, the silly feats,
Turn somersaults in leafy retreats.

So wander through these shades unseen,
Where laughter blooms amid the green.
In every sprout and unseen seam,
Lives a world that loves to dream.

Veils of Green

Among the leaves, a rabbit crows,
Hiding tales in twining rows.
Squirrels crack up, with acorn jokes,
While worms giggle, in soft-spoken pokes.

A dreaming snail, with a shell so wide,
Invents stories, with nowhere to hide.
The daisies whisper, all fluff and cheer,
Tickling the toes of those passing near.

Dandelions dance, uninvited guests,
Holding the parties that no one suggests.
A crow on a fence, with a sarcastic grin,
Claims he knows all, but forgets where he's been.

At dusk, the shadows bear witness to glee,
While pixies play hide and seek in a tree.
Each rustling leaf has a secret or two,
In this lively place, where laughter rings true.

The Enigma of Ivy

Creeping tendrils, a maze of cheer,
A raccoon's laugh, halfway up the sphere.
Tangled tales told by the vines so spry,
To the moon-washed clouds that drift on high.

Locusts hold meetings, decisions deferred,
While hippos in ponds form a band unheard.
The ivy plots mischief, with sly little twirls,
Swapping its leaves for some sparkly pearls.

A chameleon chuckles at what it might wear,
Trying on colors like it just doesn't care.
Flies gather gossip over tea made of dew,
As thorns take a break from giving their due.

At night, ivy shimmies, its dance quite absurd,
While beetles debate on the silliest word.
If walls could talk, they'd burst with delight,
Sharing the mirth in the hush of the night.

Petal-Painted Confidences

A butterfly whispers, soft as a sigh,
While tulips tell jokes with a wink and a eye.
Bees burst with laughter, as nectar they sip,
With petals as cushions, they take a quick trip.

Petals in pink gossip under the sun,
About how the daisies just don't know how to run.
A rose gives a wink, with sarcasm galore,
As a bumblebee hums at the joke from before.

Lilies trade secrets, under the moon's glare,
While creeping phlox peeks from here to there.
Tulips twirl stories and raucous delight,
In this riot of colors, everything feels right.

The daisies, delighted, decide to reprise,
All of their laughter, with pinches of spice.
In this cozy patch where secrets are spun,
Each petal and laugh brings out the fun.

Secrets of the Silent Sprout

In a quiet corner, a sprout starts to joke,
While talking to shadows, its humor bespoke.
An ant brings attention, with a silly old tale,
Measuring strength in the warmth of a gale.

Twirling round roots, a snail gives a cheer,
Mentoring each sprout, with insights sincere.
Cabbages chuckle, with their leafy retorts,
Sharing the gossip of salad-based sports.

A clump of mint laughs, 'I smell better now!'
Next to a basil that says, 'Take a bow!'
With chives in the loop, who clever and spry,
Challenge their flavors as birds fly by.

Each twitch of the green and each rustle of soil,
Becomes a stand-up act in life's simple toil.
Where quiet is comedy and sprout's just a clown,
In this whimsical patch, no one wears a frown.

Murmurs in the Thicket

In the thicket, critters talk,
Squirrels gossip as they walk.
Rabbits chuckle, owls hoot loud,
As mushrooms mingle with the crowd.

A hedgehog shares a funny tale,
Of how he slipped upon a snail.
The insects laugh, his prickles shine,
They give him snacks of sweetened twine.

A dandy lion combs his fluff,
He pretends that he's quite tough.
But when the breeze gives him a poke,
He jigs about, can't stay bespoke.

The breeze whirls in; they dance a jig,
With tiny feet, they leap and dig.
The thicket's laughter spills around,
In this wild place, joy knows no bound.

The Wisdom of Wilted Leaves.

Once a leaf, vibrant and bold,
Had dreams of glory, tales untold.
But time played tricks, and soon he knew,
With age comes wisdom, and a gentle hue.

"It's quite the art to fall with grace,"
Said a crumpled leaf in a sunny place.
If bending low is what you must,
Then let it be with style and trust.

They hold a meeting, leaves conspire,
To share their secrets by the fire.
"Who needs to stand when we can roll?"
And soon the ground was their new goal.

So when you see leaves turn to brown,
Don't doubt their fun, don't wear a frown.
For wisdom hides in crispy folds,
In every crinkle, a story unfolds.

Whispers Among the Petals

Roses giggle, tulips blush,
In the cool of evening hush.
Petals gossip, colors bright,
Trading tales 'til morning light.

A daisy asks, "What's in a name?"
The violets grin in floral fame.
"Just wear your hue with pride," they cheer,
For every blossom's charm is clear.

The marigolds dance, all ablaze,
While bees tease flowers in a daze.
"Please don't buzz too close," croaked a sprout,
"Or we might sneeze and fall right out!"

As night comes down, laughter swells,
In every bud, a joy that tells.
These whispers soft, they bloom and play,
All petals know—life's bright ballet.

Hidden Blooms of Twilight

Twilight whispers to the trees,
As flowers nod in evening breeze.
With shadows long, they hide away,
In secret spots where fairies play.

"Oh, look! A noodle-in-a-bloom!"
A silly name that made them zoom.
The petals giggle, branches sway,
As night-time mischief finds its way.

A sunflower hums a twilight tune,
While dandelion sprinkles a swoon.
"Let's scatter seeds like tiny stars,
And see who grows across the bars!"

So as the night spins dreams aglow,
Do not forget the buds that grow.
For hidden blooms are best of all,
They laugh and wiggle when darkness calls.

The Enchanted Oasis

In a patch where daisies dance,
A gopher steals a farmer's pants.
He thinks he's got a lovely prize,
But it's just a hare's disguise.

The sunflowers wear their sassy hats,
While squirrels plot their nutty chats.
A frog croaks jokes in slimy rhyme,
And all the critters laugh each time.

A butterfly with purple wings,
Claims he's the king of funny things.
He trips and falls upon a bee,
Who grumbles, "Watch out, here's my tea!"

But as the sun begins to set,
The laughter warms, we can't forget.
In this oasis, joy does bloom,
While plants hold secrets we consume.

Stories of the Silent Grove

In the grove where whispers play,
A raccoon steals the cabbages away.
He wears a hat that's far too grand,
Claiming he's the ruler of the land.

A turtle tells his tales so slow,
Of a cat who thought she'd grow.
She took a sip from the river wide,
Now she's a fish with whiskers inside!

Birds argue loudly about the trees,
A squirrel pesters, "What's the breeze?"
While mushrooms giggle with delight,
At the jester toad who leaps at night.

In this grove of wooden glee,
Creatures laugh as wild as can be.
When secrets stir beneath the leaves,
Each chuckle adds to what it weaves.

The Invisible Web

In the corner of a leafy nook,
A spider wrote a funny book.
It sells quite well to flies and more,
While wasps complain they're quite a bore.

With twisted words and tangled laughs,
The cricket spins his witty drafts.
He chirps a line, a riddle or two,
Leaves beetles guessing, feeling blue.

The ants parade in tiny shoes,
Trading stories of good and poor news.
One claims he found a giant crumb,
While others argue, "That's just dumb!"

In this realm where giggles weave,
The fun continues, can't believe!
Though secrets hide in webs so fine,
Each giggle echoes, bright as wine.

Fables Held in the Ants' Anthem

The ants, they chant their tales of gold,
Of battles fought and stories bold.
But one ant trips and lands in muck,
His friends all laugh, "Oh, what bad luck!"

In shadows dense, they scheme and plot,
As one of them reveals the pot.
A treasure found, a crumb so sweet,
But it's just stale bread from their last feast!

A wise old snail just chews his leaf,
While others giggle at their grief.
"My time is slow," he starts to sing,
"But laughter makes me sprout my wings."

In this anthem of the tiny throng,
Each secret shared is full of song.
So let them dance and let them sway,
For in their world, it's a funny play.

Enigma of the Evening Bloom

In the twilight's soft embrace,
Frogs hold court in leafy space.
Whispers dance on dewy leaves,
Telling tales the night believes.

A snail's race is quite the sight,
He wears his shell, a fancy light.
Beetles boast of evening's sway,
While crickets join the wild ballet.

The moon peeks through, a cheeky grin,
As flowers giggle, let the fun begin.
Petals sway, with secrets to share,
In this comical, fragrant air.

A rabbit dons a hat of green,
Declares himself the garden's queen.
With every hop, he spreads delight,
In the revelry of fleeting night.

Hidden Glimmers

Underneath the twisted vine,
A gnome is sipping herbal wine.
He winks and then begins to hum,
While fireflies join, oh what a drum!

The daisies wear their polka dots,
And swaying trees connect the spots.
A squirrel juggles acorns near,
Prompted by a gust of cheer.

A puddle mirrors a bouncing star,
As beetles dance upon a jar.
Butterflies trade their silly hats,
Chasing shadows, barking at chat!

Laughter echoed from the blooms,
As daisies huddled in their rooms.
Each giggle shared among the green,
Makes the night a merry scene.

The Hidden Grove

In the shade of ancient trees,
A turtle jokes, saying, "I'm free!"
With every step, he takes a bow,
To all who pass, "You're just like me now!"

The mushrooms whisper silly rhymes,
As laughter rings through market times.
A hedgehog wears a little tie,
Pretending he can reach the sky!

In this grove of quirky cheer,
The air is sweet, the path is clear.
Small wonders hide in every nook,
Just take a peek—go on, look!

An owl is serving tea at dusk,
While breezes chuckle, cool and brisk.
With every sip, a riddle flows,
In this grove where laughter grows.

Ghosts of the Garden Path

The shadows stroll on cobblestone,
While garden gnomes clap, stoned and prone.
They hoot in jest, a ghostly cheer,
As moonlit figures disappear.

A spider weaves a joke so tight,
"Who's the best at frightful flight?"
The wind replies with gentle nudges,
As daisies shake with joyful judges.

With every rustle, smiles ignite,
Phantom roses bloom with delight.
Their petals giggle, soft and bright,
In shadows cast by playful light.

And if you wander down this way,
Prepare for laughs, come what may.
For in this realm of secret craft,
The spirits giggle at every draft.

Nectar's Quiet Embrace

In a bloom's sweet whisper, I'd sneak a taste,
The honeybees dance, it's a sugary race.
Petals giggle softly as they catch the sun,
A sip of their laughter, oh this life is fun!

The daisies tell tales in the warm, bright air,
A rivalry sparked between roses and flair.
"I'm the prettiest!" they shout with delight,
While thorns roll their eyes, oh what a sight!

Butterflies flutter by, wearing silly hats,
While ants march along, discussing their stats.
"Who stole my pollen?" grumbled Mr. Bee,
A buzzing detective, as funny as can be!

So here in this realm, the blooms play their part,
Each petal a player in Nature's own art.
With laughter and joy, they swirl in their glee,
In this secretive land, where they're wild and free!

The Secret Keeper of Ivy

Ivy creeps softly, with gossip to share,
Whispers of rabbits, and what's in their lair.
"Did you hear that, friend?" she slyly exclaims,
"Tadpoles in tap shoes are dancing in games!"

The snails have a party, but oh what a fuss,
They wear tiny hats, each one made of rust.
"Let's race to that leaf!" yells the fastest one,
But they barely move, oh what a slow fun!

Mice hold a meeting beneath the big tree,
Discussing their cheese and what they will see.
"A slice for a friend is a slice twice the charm!"
They squeak and they giggle in each other's arms!

With ivy's green tendrils, they weave and they play,
Life's silly antics unfold every day.
Secrets are safe, in this whimsical keep,
Where laughter and fun are the dreams that we reap!

Beneath the Glade

Beneath the old oak, the shadows do sway,
The squirrels tell stories of bright autumn days.
"I found a nut once!" one boldly declares,
While others just shrug, with nuts combed in hair!

The mushrooms all huddle, with caps quite tall,
Debating the weather, "Will it rain or stall?"
"I'd rather not drown!" shouts the brave toadstool,
As a raindrop slips in, oh what a cool pool!

Crickets perform as the sun starts to fade,
They chirp out a tune like a lively parade.
"Dance, little fireflies, twinkle in flight!"
But some just blink lazily, avoiding the light.

In this glade of wonders, each critter's a star,
With charades and loud laughter, they all raise the bar.
So here in this haven, let the joy cascade,
For moments of fun are the treasures we've made!

Unraveled Vines of Memory

Vines twist and tangle, in a jumbled delight,
Remembering old tales by the moon's silver light.
"I once climbed so high, but I must have been small!"
"Did you bring a snack?" asks a sprightly green ball!

The flowers confide in a mix-up parade,
While daisies and dandelions color the shade.
"Do you think I'm taller?" one blossom debates,
But the others all giggle, as they share their traits.

A wise old sunflower grins, saying with cheer,
"Don't fret about height, it's the vibes that we steer!"
As bees buzz around with their transactional drone,
Passing gossip like candy, the sweetest of tone!

In this woven chaos of nature's own chat,
Laughter and stories are where it is at.
So let's twine our memories, with smiles on display,
Life's funny as ever, in this magical play!

Secrets in the Breeze

The daisies whisper tales of bees,
Who stole their nectar with such ease.
But in the wind, they giggle bold,
For every flower has stories told.

The rose pricks secrets, sharp and sly,
While daisies dance and wave goodbye.
The tulips play a game of hide,
As raindrops tumble down with pride.

The sunflowers nod with knowing smiles,
Confetti petals line their aisles.
They chuckle soft, in hues so bright,
About the moon's mischief at night.

In the breeze, the laughter flows,
Of hidden truths that nobody knows.
A playful tune, this floral tease,
With every gust, it sways with ease.

The Buried Song of Roots

Beneath the soil where whispers play,
The roots are singing all day.
With tuba beats and trumpet leaves,
They groan in glee as laughter weaves.

Worms tap dance, they think they're slick,
While seedlings bob, they sing their trick.
Oh, what a show, beneath the ground,
In a crusty harmony, they abound.

Grubs hold maracas, shaking bright,
As ants groove on, what a delight!
But shh! Keep quiet, it's their refrain,
No creature must hear the silly pain.

With dirt as stage and sun as spotlight,
Roots twist and twirl, oh what a sight!
A melody of muck, so absurd,
But oh, the laughter, it can't be heard!

Visions Through the Pansies

Pansies giggle in hues so bold,
Wearing faces, stories unfold.
One winks at bees, another sighs,
With petals painted like the skies.

The violets laugh at prying eyes,
While shadows peek where mischief lies.
Frogs join in, croaking their cheer,
Critters convene when no one's near.

But oh, the daisies, sweet but coy,
Stash secrets like a hidden toy.
They nudge and natter, as if in glee,
Whispering truths that none can see.

Through pansy frames, the daydreams peek,
In a floral realm, where whispers speak.
With laughter bright, they live and sway,
Concealing jest in bright bouquet!

The Hidden Path

A path of stones that twist and turn,
Hides giggles soft, waiting to discern.
The ferns are flirts in playful fray,
While hedgehogs prance the winding way.

With thorns and thistles acting shy,
The trees above just wave goodbye.
But a hidden nook there lies along,
Where even turtles hum a tune of song.

The butterflies glide, with whims to share,
An amusing map of scents and flair.
Rabbits race but never tire,
For laughter fuels their leap and choir.

Through twists of grass, a joy parade,
Unfolds within the leafy shade.
So follow the laughter, loose and light,
On this joyous path, where fun takes flight!

Whispers Among the Petals

In the tulips, a gossip takes flight,
Roses blushing, overhear at night.
Daisies giggle at the fanciest tales,
While sneaky vines peek at the snails.

Caterpillars dance on a leaf so green,
With each twirl, a new joke is seen.
The sunflowers sway, hands on their hips,
While butterflies plot their party trips.

Bumblebees buzz with a sassy tune,
Teasing the ants, "We'll be here till noon!"
The petals chuckle at the buzzing spree,
Who knew bloom time could be so free?

In this patch, laughter never ends,
Speaking in colors, the blooms make amends.
Together they sprout, in mischief and glee,
Each day a secret shared, just wait and see.

The Hidden Boughs

Under thick branches, where shadows play,
Squirrels share tales of a mischievous day.
They hide their acorns with utmost care,
Only to forget - what a woodland affair!

A woodpecker taps, "Do you hear the news?
The raccoons are staging a midnight snooze!"
The leaves rustle softly, with whispers so sly,
A chorus of laughter as the owls flutter by.

"What's that over there?" chirps a brave sparrow,
"It's just the wind or maybe a pharaoh!"
Beneath the boughs, they plot and they scheme,
Each hidden nook is a sweet little dream.

With cheeky grins, they all take a stand,
Playing hide and seek in this leafy land.
Through branches they giggle, their secrets unfold,
In the hidden boughs, funny stories are told.

Secrets Beneath the Leaves

Tucked under foliage, whispers swirl,
A ladybug laughs, as a leaf unfurls.
"Did you see Sally, with glittery spots?"
Toads by the pond giggle at their thoughts.

A snail struts by, with a shell so bright,
Saying, "Slow and steady will win me the fight!"
The mushrooms chuckle, under soft light,
"What about Gary? He's quite a sight!"

The frogs in harmony croak out a song,
While beetles roll dice, all night long.
Secrets exchanged 'neath the leafy dome,
Each jest a promise: we'll never roam.

In this bustling world, where whispers abound,
Every beetle has stories that can astound.
So come closer now, and bend down to hear,
The giggles and grins that are ever so near.

Silent Blooms in Shadow

In the twilight hush, blooms softly gleam,
Petals share shadows, weaving a dream.
"Oh look at that!" a violet exclaims,
As daisies ponder on their silly names.

The lilies giggle as they sway in the breeze,
Telling the poppies, "We're born to tease!"
While nightingales sing, the garden takes flight,
With secretive laughs that dance through the night.

A grumpy old fern huffs at the jest,
"Keep it down, you lively pests!"
But the blooms just chuckle, and softly reply,
"We'll sprout more giggles before we say bye!"

So when dusk falls, and laughter is thick,
Remember the blooms, each giggle a trick.
In the dark, they shine, with petals aglow,
Silent blooms in shadow, putting on a show.

The Unseen Oasis

In the quiet corner, where gnomes tend to hide,
Lies a fountain of giggles in the grass, so wide.
It bubbles with laughter, trickles with cheer,
A splash here and there, let's toast with a sneer!

Whispers of daisies tease the snoozing bees,
Poking their stingers at the tickling breeze.
Who knew that the shrubs could throw such a bash?
With sprightly green limbs and a dash of panache!

The squirrels throw a party with acorn delights,
While the frogs in the pond stage their croaky rights.
Everyone's invited, except for the cat,
She dances on rooftops and just rolls for a nap!

So chase down the shadows and frolic with joy,
In this realm of the wild where no one's a ploy.
A twist of the vines and a tickle of thyme,
A merry brigade that won't pay any crime!

Sprouts of Mystery

What's growing in silence, curled up in a leaf?
A hat made of noodles, you'd faint in disbelief!
The sunbeams wiggle, and the shadows conspire,
To brew magic potions from twigs and some fire.

The carrots wear glasses, and the radishes dance,
While the pumpkins gossip about who has a chance.
Each tomato embarks on a journey, bold and bright,
Claiming that twilight was made just for flight!

On teacups of petals, the ladybugs sip,
Throwing confetti in a cloud of sweet dip.
The garlic's so charming with tales that it weaves,
Of garlic bulb kingdoms tucked under the leaves.

So wander this wonder, with glee in your stride,
Where sprouts chuckle softly, and secrets can't hide.
Each twig is a riddle, each flower a grin,
In this patch of confusion, let the fun begin!

Beneath the Surface

Beneath the thin soil, a circus unfolds,
Worms don sequined jackets and tell tales of old.
A mole in a tuxedo, so snazzy and spry,
Juggles acorns like treasures, oh my, oh my!

The roots have a meeting, discussing their plot,
They're planning a heist for the sun with a knot.
While radishes plot with their spicy reprise,
To tickle the turnips and give them a surprise!

The beetles, they bicker over who's the best dressed,
While snails claim their bling is not just for jest.
"I'll win with my shimmer," said one with a grin,
As the earthworms roll dice, let the games begin!

So dive down below, where the wild things rave,
And the laughter reverberates deep in the cave.
Each giggle brings wonders that ripple the earth,
In the sprightly domain where all laughter gives birth.

The Language of Dandelions

The dandelions chat in a language of fluff,
They scatter their secrets just when times get tough.
Whispers of yellow float up to the sun,
With wishes of laughter, oh goodness, such fun!

A puff and a breeze sends their messages far,
As they plot with the daisies to open a bar.
With cocktails of nectar and snacks made of dew,
They toast to the critters that come for a chew!

Their roots hold a treasure of chuckles and tales,
Of pranks played on rabbits and adventurous snails.
"Let's dance in the moonlight," the dandelions cry,
While the wind makes them twirl, just so long and so high!

Unruly and merry, they rise with the dust,
Reminding us all that grow where you must.
In fields full of giggles that sparkle and shine,
Join hands with the daisies; let's sip on good wine!

The Moonflower's Secret

At midnight's call, she wakes to dance,
In shadows' glow, she takes her chance.
Her petals yawn, a silvery grin,
Whispers of mischief, let the fun begin!

The bees in tuxedos, all dressed so neat,
Tap dance on blossoms, a floral treat.
They sip sweet nectar, play a bold game,
While moonlight giggles, calling their name.

Thrumming with Life

Crickets compose their nightly song,
Ants parade by, they march along.
Ladybugs launch a daring flight,
In this lively night, oh what a sight!

Daisies in frocks spin round and round,
While roly-polys jam on the ground.
Squirrels in top hats take a bow,
Dancing with shadows, time to wow!

The Celestial Blossom

A flower with dreams that reach for the sky,
It winks at the stars, oh my, oh my!
Dressed in pajamas, it fluffs and sways,
A secret routine in moonlight's rays.

Comets giggle as they zoom by,
The blossom winks back, oh why not try?
It molds and bounces, like playful clay,
Revealing its charm in a comical way!

Fables of the Fern

Ferns tell tales in the softest green,
Of gnomes and shadows, quite the scene.
With curls and twists, they mock and tease,
In laughter's embrace, they sway with ease.

They boast of wisdom, ancient and bold,
While tickling toes, their stories unfold.
In the whispers of leaves, a chuckle erupts,
For secrets of ferns can never be bluffed!

The Dancer on the Breeze

A butterfly twirled, in a coat of bright hues,
Spinning around, in a whimsical snooze.
She sneezed a petal, that landed with flair,
And startled a snail, who was lost in his care.

The flowers all giggled, shaking their heads,
While bees buzzed with laughter, weaving their threads.
A breeze played the tune, and they danced with glee,
Who knew nature's waltz was so silly, you see?

Petals that Hold Their Breath

In the shade of the blooms, quite a drama unfolds,
A secret affair, or so rumor holds.
The petals all whisper, 'shh! Don't you dare!'
As a ladybug flirts, with a confident air.

But the daisies just chuckle, eyes rolling in jest,
'He's such a pretender, he's not quite the best!'
They hold their breaths tightly, in sun's golden light,
Waiting for love to take off in flight.

A Symphony of Soil

The earthworms compose, with their squiggly tunes,
Complaining about roots, and pesky raccoons.
Their concert is vibrant; it goes on for days,
Yet only the daisies know how to play.

A cat starts to yawn, in the back of the crowd,
As the mushrooms do jazz, all gloomy and proud.
The ants tap their feet, in a line that's so neat,
While the toad croaks along, with a slightly off beat!

The Keeper of the Gate

A gnome on the top, with a hat full of tricks,
Claims he knows all the wildflower's licks.
He keeps watch at night with a wink and a grin,
Making sure no one sneaks in for a win.

But who's that sneaking, with their feet oh so light?
A raccoon in shadows, planning a bite!
The gnome shouts 'Stop! This is my little show!'
While the raccoon just chuckles, and scurries below.

Flickering Imprints

There once was a gnome named Lou,
He painted his toes a bright hue.
The flowers turned heads,
They're gossiping spreads,
About how his toenails just grew.

A squirrel wore shades made of pine,
Sipping acorns like fine wine.
He danced on the grass,
With moves that surpassed,
While flowers all giggled in line.

The hedgehogs played poker at dusk,
With bets made from leaves and old husk.
Yet one took a nap,
In a flower's soft lap,
Leaving everyone puzzled and husk.

So next time you peek through the leaves,
Remember what silliness weaves.
For laughter can sprout,
In the quirkiest route,
Where nature and whimsy believes.

Shadows Dwell in Flora

In shadows where daisies do hide,
A snail claimed he'd take a big stride.
He slipped on a leaf,
Cried out in disbelief,
And now has a snail shell to ride.

The frogs in the pond sing off-key,
With harmonies fit for a spree.
They croak up a storm,
In a lyrical form,
While the lilies just roll in glee.

A worm thought he'd join in the fun,
He wiggled and danced in the sun.
But he tripped on a root,
And landed quite cute,
Now he's known as the wriggly one.

So next time you wonder who plays,
In the bright light of sunshine and rays,
Just peek at the floor,
You'll find laughs galore,
In this world where silliness stays.

The Language of Dandelions

Dandelions spoke to the bees,
Whispering sweetly with ease.
They promised a treat,
Of pollen so neat,
But ended up stuck in the breeze.

A rabbit thought he was quite sly,
He donned a dandelion tie.
But when he skipped by,
With a wink in his eye,
He tickled a skunk on the thigh.

The clovers conspired in green,
To prank all who came in between.
With a giggle and sway,
They led folks astray,
To a patch where no grass could be seen.

So next time you spy a bright bloom,
Remember the laughter can loom.
In patches so wild,
Like a mischievous child,
Nature's humor can lift up the gloom.

Secrets Woven in Vines

In corners where ivy does creep,
There's gossip the critters can keep.
A spider spun tales,
Of epic weight fails,
While whispers of secrets still leap.

The butterflies flaunt like they're stars,
With patterns like stripes from guitars.
They flutter and preen,
In their patterns so clean,
Maybe seeking to charm some new cars.

The tomatoes have tales filled with zest,
Of who is the juiciest guest.
They roll with delight,
In the soft moonlight,
And treasure the glee of their jest.

So if you should wander where green,
And laughter in nature's seen,
Know every vine,
And each twist and line,
Holds secrets of joy to glean.

Nature's Hidden Narratives

In a patch of weeds, a gnome takes a nap,
Dreaming of veggies and a sunburnt cap.
A squirrel tells tales of the day he stole,
An acorn so big, it rolled like a ball.

The daisies gossip as the wind weaves through,
About a shy butterfly that lost a shoe.
Pansies chuckle at the bee's awkward dance,
While cucumbers wonder if they stand a chance.

A worm in the soil holds the juiciest news,
About the last party that ended in blues.
The carrots chuckle, "Now who's got the sauce?"
As radishes roll their eyes and toss.

Underneath the leaves, secrets fill the air,
A frog plays a tune, with a flair so rare.
Each petal and root has a story to share,
Where laughter blooms, without a care.

The Tapestry of Foliage

The shrubs are bustling with gossip and cheer,
A cat sneaks around, shh! Do you hear?
The roses are plotting a grand little scheme,
To transform the garden into a beauty dream.

The vines stretch out, telling tales in the breeze,
Of flowers that loved to tickle the bees.
A daffodil winks at a passing young snail,
While daisies debate who can squeak the loudest yell.

In the patch, a hedgehog is hosting a game,
With mushrooms as seats, oh, isn't it lame?
They chuckle and giggle at the snail's slow roll,
As the wind tells stories of a nearby shoal.

Plant friends unite under moon's silver glow,
With whispers that burst, then quickly bestow.
In every green corner, laughter's the rule,
As they gather 'round for a night of pure cool.

Shadows of the Flower Bed

In the corner, a daisy plays hide-and-seek,
While sunflowers strut, so tall and unique.
Beneath leafy canopies where secrets are spun,
Mischief is brewing, oh, this will be fun!

A mushroom declares he's the brightest of all,
While the tulips roll eyes, thinking he's small.
The petunias gossip about a bug on a leaf,
Claiming it's dressed up as some kind of chief.

A ladybug chirps, "I'm moving today!"
While the gardens agree he could go any way.
The shadows are dancing, making jokes on the sly,
As the plants break out in a collective sigh.

With rustles and giggles, the petals unite,
To share all the secrets of day turned to night.
Amidst blooms and buds, laughter rises like bread,
In the shadows, they've found all the fun to be fed.

Mysteries of the Meadow

In a meadow so bright, the daisies convene,
Hatching plans for a party that's fit for a queen.
Butterflies whisper of a new dance in style,
While the grass tickles toes with a cheeky smile.

A rabbit plays coy, hiding behind a bush,
Eavesdropping on chickens who argue and hush.
"Why's that beet so grumpy, is it late for a date?"
While the daisies laugh, "Just wait for the fate!"

Foxgloves are flirting with the clouds way up high,
Bragging about how they can touch the blue sky.
A cricket hops in with a joke on his tongue,
"Why don't flowers sing? 'Cause they're too well hung!"

The sun dips down, painting stories in gold,
Whispers of laughter from the young and the old.
Each critter and bloom has a tale to enact,
In a meadow of merriment, that's a funny fact.

www.ingramcontent.com/pod-product-compliance
Lightning Source LLC
Chambersburg PA
CBHW052221090526
44585CB00015BA/1410